合氣道 LIVING
AIKIDO

LIVING
AIKIDO

BY

BRUCE KLICKSTEIN

UNDER THE SUPERVISION OF
MORIHIRO SAITO

NORTH ATLANTIC BOOKS
BERKELEY, CALIFORNIA

Living Aikido

Copyright © 1987 by Bruce Klickstein

ISBN 0–938190–85–7 (paperback)
ISBN 0–938190–86–5 (cloth)

Published by North Atlantic Books
2800 Woolsey Street
Berkeley, California 94705

Cover and technique photos by Wolfgang Baumgartner
Cover and book design by Paula Morrison
Typeset by Classic Typography

Living Aikido is sponsored by the Society for the Study
of Native Arts and Sciences, a nonprofit educational
corporation whose goals are to develop an ecological and
crosscultural perspective linking various scientific, social,
and artistic fields; to nurture a holistic view of arts,
sciences, humanities, and healing; and to publish and
distribute literature on the relationship of mind, body,
and nature.

Library of Congress Cataloging-in-Publication Data

Klickstein, Bruce, 1953–
    Living aikido.

    Bibliography: p.
    1. Aikido—Training.   I. Saitō, Morihiro.   II. Title.
GV1114.35.K55   1987   796.8′154   86–33123
ISBN 0–938190–86–5
ISBN 0–938190–85–7 (pbk.)

CONTENTS

Dedicated to

MORIHEI UESHIBA

the dream of aikido,
the discipline which made it real,
and the willingness to share it with the world.

ACKNOWLEDGEMENTS

It is said that progress in aikido is a matter of your own commitment and training. In fact, you depend a great deal on fellow students, senior students, and the sensei for support and inspiration. Many people give selflessly of their time, knowledge, body, and soul towards your growth.

I could not begin writing this book on aikido without expressing my gratitude to my teacher, Morihiro Saito Sensei.

For 24 years he devoted himself as an apprentice to the Founder of aikido. To this day Saito Sensei continues to train daily even after forty years of training. Ever since the Founder passed away in 1969, Saito Sensei, together with his wife, has continued to care for the Aiki Shrine and the Founder's dojo in Iwama. He feels his responsibility to be that of preserving aikido in its traditional form, as the Founder taught it in Iwama, and to extend this teaching to aikido communities around the world.

It is difficult to adequately express my appreciation for his years of dedication, patience, severe training, and selfless teaching. My way of saying thank you to him for all he has given to me is to follow his example and share it with great spirit. I also wish to thank him specifically for his not-so-gentle suggestion to write this book.

And I also wish to thank my students for their dedication and love of aikido. They make my life very rich.

My gratitude to George Leonard for his enthusiasm and support; Pat Hendricks, Hoa Nguyen, Wolfgang Baumgartner, Peter Slote, Art Ward, Richard Grossinger, Paula Morrison, Kim Peuser, and my wife Sally Klickstein for help on the production of this book; Stan Pranin of *Aiki News* for the biographical information and special photographs of the Founder; my parents; and a special appreciation to Frank Doran and Bill Witt for their friendship.

岩間合気修練道場　道場長八段　斉藤守弘
１９８６年９月１７日

　此度、ブルース君が本を出版されることに対して、私は心からお祝い申し上げます。ブルース君は開祖が合気道を完成させた道場、そして合気神社のある岩間に、自ら修行の場と心に決めて来日し、私のもとで、七度び、長期間にわたり懸命に修行を続けました。才能ある彼は遂に岩間に残した開祖直々の練習方式に依り、基本から段階的にその技を習得しました。そして、彼は礼節を重んずる私の最高級の門下生であります。剣・杖・体術の理合を習得した現在の彼は、優秀な指導者であることは勿論、これからの合気道界を背負っていく、私の最も期待する人物の一人であります。そして、ブルース君のこの本は、初心者にとって誤りのない方向を示しており、有段者にとっても誤りを修正することの出来る本格的指導書であります。現在の合気道は、多くの指導者に依り新しい技法が沢山発表されております。しかし、その中で迷わず開祖の教えを守り続ける彼の姿は尊く美しく見えます。この本により、多くの人々が伝統的合気道を依り一層理解して戴けることを心からお祈り申し上げる次第です。

FOREWORD BY
MORIHIRO SAITO
8TH DAN, CHIEF INSTRUCTOR, IWAMA DOJO

On this occasion, the publication of Bruce's book, I wish to offer my heartfelt congratulations. The dojo in Iwama, located near the Aiki Shrine, is where the Founder completed the development of Aikido. It was to this place that Bruce's heart led him to serve his apprenticeship. He has been here seven times; under my direct guidance he has persevered through long, severe, and disciplined study.

Thanks to his talent, and to the training methods taught directly by the Founder in Iwama, Bruce eventually acquired the knowledge of the stages of technique as a progression from the basic forms. He has a high regard for etiquette and is one of my most advanced students. He has an up-to-date knowledge of the relationships between ken, jo, and tai-jutsu. It goes without saying that he is an excellent instructor and I have high hopes that he will become one of the pillars of the Aikido world.

Free of error, Bruce's book is both a reliable guide for beginners and, for yudansha, an authentic reference book to be used in the correction of their own technique.

Many instructors are creating many new techniques, but among them, Bruce's form, which continues to preserve clearly the teachings of the Founder, is valuable and beautiful to see.

I sincerely pray that, through this book, many people will come to understand traditional Aikido.

photo by Jerry A. Green

FOREWORD BY
GEORGE LEONARD

For the millions of people who have been attracted to the Oriental martial arts in recent decades, aikido presents a fascinating paradox. Its stance is non-combative. Its most fundamental response to attack involves seeing the world from the attacker's viewpoint. And its ultimate aim is love, harmony, the end of conflict and war. All this in an art that is known for the effectiveness of its control techniques and the irresistible power of its throws. To deepen the mystery, aikido confronts the martial artist with a bewildering array of physical moves. Within certain basic principles, in fact, its techniques and variations are infinite.

The upshot is that many people, drawn to aikido for its philosophy and its spiritual qualities, are unable to find their bearings and soon drop out. Even advanced students are often at a loss for words and concepts through which they might explain and appreciate their art. True understanding of aikido demands years of dedicated practice. Still, there is a need for a book that can serve as a guide to its mysteries, a book that is simple and clear enough to aid the student in his or her daily physical practice and, at the same time, one possessing the depth and breadth to inform that practice as it applies to every aspect of living.

Now Bruce Klickstein, one of America's most highly regarded aikidoists and the chief instructor of the Aikido Institute of Oakland, has given us such a book. Klickstein began the practice of aikido in 1968 at age fourteen. He has studied intensively in the U.S. and Japan, and has presented his approach to the art at numerous high-level seminars throughout the U.S. and overseas. Today, at 32, he holds a 5th degree black belt. He is one of the youngest Americans ever to hold that rank.

In *Living Aikido*, Bruce Klickstein distills aikido's infinite techniques and variations down to five essential forms:

> Ikkyo
> Shiho-nage
> Irimi-nage
> Kokyu-nage
> Koshi-nage

Each of these forms or techniques is presented in detail through words and pictures as an aid to training. But there is more. Klickstein sees each technique as manifesting a unique quality or *character*. Ikkyo's character, for example, is *connectedness*, and one's sincere practice of ikkyo in its many variations both reflects and is reflected in one's sense of connectedness in daily life.

For Klickstein, the techniques are not static qualities but ever-changing opportunities for personal growth and development. Each is the manifestation of a profound and eternal essence, which manifests in the world of space, time, and momentum as a process. Through sincere practice, the aikidoist may participate in this process and become involved in lifelong discovery.

For years, students have asked me, "What book on aikido can I read to help me in my practice?" I thank Bruce Klickstein for giving me an answer.

INTRODUCTION

Come to the edge
    no we'll fall
Come to the edge
    no we can't
Come to the edge
    no we're afraid
and they came
and he pushed them
and they flew

Aikido is a unique and still relatively young martial art. Created and developed in the early 1900's by Morihei Ueshiba in Japan, it is both a totally practical martial art, and at the same time so powerful in its ability to bring transformation into its practitioners' lives that it almost needs another name to describe what it truly is.

Training in aikido is complex. There are a great many skills, techniques, principles, and attitudes to be studied and synthesized into a single understanding called aikido. Traditionally, there exists a step-by-step methodology that will guide the student steadily from the early stages of training to more advanced levels.

It is my concern with the current popularity and rapid growth in aikido, that future students and teachers will have the knowledge of the traditional basic techniques and methods that form the foundation for substantial growth in aikido.

At its source, aikido is a budo, a "martial way." As a budo, it is more than a

the Founder in front of the Iwama dojo

group of practical combat techniques, though it is a very effective self-defense form. Aikido works in the realm of human and spiritual development. It is not just a martial art that has a philosophical base or a spiritual side attached. Nor is it a spiritual creed with a physical form attached. The techniques and philosophy of aikido can no more be separated than two sides of a coin. A nickel can be cut in two halves, heads from tails, but it isn't worth five cents any more. Separate the form from the spirit of aikido, and you end up with neither. The techniques and the philosophy are one.

Conceptualizing about aikido out of the context of training is a practice wrought with pitfalls, which only increases the possibility of misunderstanding some of aikido's fundamental principles. A description of an object and the real object are not the same thing.

The concept of aiki principles is like a picture of a bowl of rice. You would not be satisfied eating a picture of a bowl of rice, nor will you be satisfied just having the idea of aikido in your head. A real bowl of rice is nourishing and so is the real aiki when it is alive in your body and spirit. The concept that is aikido is learned and expressed through the techniques of aikido. The philosophy of aikido comes to life only when you practice it and live it.

Therefore, the purpose of this book is not to discuss the philosophy of aikido but to outline a basic process through which you can enhance your training and experience the benefit of this art by virtue of your own practice.

There is no easy way to bring together the realms of form and spirit in a way that is true to both. For it to be truly aikido, the form must have integrity as a martial art, while the spirit must remain true to the principles of aiki, universal harmony. And they both must be true to each other without compromising the integrity of either.

Both words, aikido and budo, end with the syllable "do," which means "way" or "path." A "way" clearly implies that it is not just a series of skills to be learned and performed, but a process that permeates your daily life. Deep involvement on the path means that training will delve into areas of form, motion, attitudes, habits, spiritual ideals, and human relations. And it is through daily training in aikido techniques that clear insight into these areas of study develops.

Mastery of aikido is a journey, not a destination. To attain that condition of

calligraphy by the Founder

in front of the old Aiki shrine

being in which philosophy, technique, attitude, and spirit merge requires consistent, sincere training. There are no shortcuts.

The joining of spirit and technique is inherent in aikido, yet a number of prerequisites exist before this unity will manifest itself in a student. The form must be impeccable and strong. The spirit must be hungry and open, searching. There must be the willingness and faith to renounce old ways of moving and being for the possibility of discovering new and wonderful skills and perceptions within yourself.

This book is not meant in any way to replace a teacher. Proper development in aikido requires guidance, discipline, and support from someone who has a deep knowledge of its various aspects.

What I hope to cover in these pages is how our understanding of technique and principle develops through different stages as we train and grow. This book has been written as an exploration into my own training and into the knowledge passed on from my teacher. This search is ongoing, and the reader who wishes to reap the maximum benefit from this book will read it in this spirit, as a catalyst for training.

My hope here is to offer support to beginners who have just started on the path and beginners who have been training for a long time.

If any message summarizes these chapters, it is this: think, feel, and inquire deeply into every part of your practice; train with your whole body, mind, and spirit, letting every atom in your being be a part of every move; and train with great joy.

the Founder and Morihiro Saito in Iwama

the Aiki shrine

the Iwama dojo

Saito Sensei receiving a certificate of appreciation and an American flag from the U.S. ambassador to Japan.

Saito Sensei at a workshop at Lake Tahoe, California.

The author in front of the Iwama dojo.

TRAINING

Dream in light years
Challenge miles
Walk step by step

Aikido is at once a sophisticated, complex art, and at the same time, a simple way of relating to motion and energy. At the beginning, you simply have to come to the dojo and train. In a short while, your understanding of aikido will become increasingly complex, with a deep understanding of its myriad relationships and implications. Your training will reflect this. You will know hundreds of techniques and thousands of variations. Later, as your understanding of the art deepens, you will become as a beginner again, realizing that growth in aikido is a matter of simply showing up in the dojo and training.

To follow are some of the different aspects, attitudes, and practices that set the stage for aikido training. They are presented separately here for ease of explanation. In reality, they are quite intertwined.

An explanation of an idea sometimes supports and sometimes hinders true experience of the subject. If something here enhances training and supports a deep knowing within yourself, wonderful. TRAIN. If you are confused by something written here, don't dwell on it. TRAIN. You will understand when it is time to understand.

PROCESS OF TRAINING

There is a natural process involved in learning and growing in aikido. You begin by practicing small parts of techniques and principles, then you put some of the parts together and try to make them work smoothly as a whole movement. Often the parts work well but fall apart when the whole technique is attempted. Gradually, your understanding of the parts and of the whole will merge. The realization that this is a natural process will allow you to focus on one aspect of aikido and not worry about the aspects you are not working on. Trying to "get it all now," is equivalent to learning to juggle starting with seven balls. You end up dropping them all. Start with one, then two, then three, and soon you will be able to pay attention to the overall motion instead of trying to catch each one.

Be patient. You may focus mainly on hip movements for a few weeks, then work on foot movements, then study the relationship of aiki sword and body arts. An understanding of aiki and of how the different aspects of training fit together will develop when all of the pieces are ready, and not a moment sooner.

BEING A BEGINNER

The first step in learning anything is to say the words "I don't know." When you say them as a brand new student, you learn. When you say them again after many years of training, at that moment you learn again. When you consider yourself an expert, your cup is filled with old knowledge and there is little room for more. The purpose of training in a dojo is for discovery, for growth, not for performance of what you already know.

For aikido to be effective in a person's life, the techniques and principles must be second nature. The process of taking a shallow understanding of a technique and making it a natural, integrated part of you happens through endless repetition. This repetition must not be empty and mindless. Each iteration of a technique must be filled with your whole being. One million repetitions multiplied by zero equals zero. One thousand times one is one thousand. It is by practicing a technique over and over, with your full attention, that understanding and ability develop.

We all have the tendency to judge ourselves. I'm good, I'm bad, I'm better than. . . . It is important to be able to evaluate ourselves honestly. In order to progress, we need the information that a technique worked or was a struggle or was choppy or that we were off balance. But this is different from judging. When we evaluate, we take the information, apply it to the practice at hand, and continue training. We value this information equally whether it is flattering or not. When we judge, we tend to get stuck at the moment of judging and stay stuck in our ego's feeling proud of a well-executed technique or bad for a poor one. Our progress stops. Growth in aikido is continuous. The only time it stops is when we judge it. Keep training.

Much more is happening than mere

progress in your ability to perform a technique. Through training, your sensitivity, awareness, stamina, and centeredness are all being trained. If you should begin to feel that your techniques have deteriorated, it might be that your awareness has increased and you have become aware of things that you previously didn't notice. If a technique feels good, it's possible that your awareness is down and you aren't being sensitive to your mistakes. Trying to judge your own progress is like trying to look into your own eyes without a mirror. Don't waste the few moments you have in the dojo. Put your heart into training and you will progress.

There are really no good students or bad students of aikido. Only those who are alive in discovery and training and those who are not.

VISION/REALITY

Our ability to see is often colored by how we want or expect things to be. We expect someone to strike at our stomach so we don't see the real strike coming at our head. When the sensei is executing a technique we have seen countless times, we often reach into our inner library of techniques and play our own tapes of how we know the technique is done. We don't see the real technique as the teacher demonstrates it at that moment. So we may miss something of great value.

Learn to perceive motion as it really is. Question, "How is he really holding? How is she really moving her feet?" Answer these simple questions and you will begin to develop a deeper perception of how things really are, unclouded by preconceptions and expectations.

Practice watching each time as if it were the very first time you had ever seen the technique. Be aware: this is very difficult.

ETIQUETTE/REIGI

Like the practice of aikido techniques, etiquette trains the spirit through the observance of outward forms. Etiquette is that aspect of aikido training that specifically addresses safety, mutual trust, and respect, along with physical, mental and spiritual openness—in short, the attitudes and conditions that make up an environment conducive to growth in aikido.

There is great value in the knowledge and power offered to you by the sensei and fellow students. Learning often happens in unexpected ways, at unexpected times; it may come to you from a beginner as well as from a sensei. Etiquette is a way for you to make ready and stay ready for that learning.

The bow that you give to the shomen—the symbol of the spirit of the Founder, of aikido itself, and all aikidoka—affirms your gratitude to those whose efforts to learn have made it possible for you to learn. The bow that you give your sensei is also one of gratitude, and, more than just that, one of continuing trust and the willingness to keep your mind and spirit open to new learning. Finally, the bow between you and your training partner affirms the mutual gratitude, mutual trust, and mutual respect involved in your efforts to learn and help each other grow in aikido. Without this trust and respect, something would always be lacking in your training. Both you and your partner might well hold back, tighten up, and worry about protecting your bodies or egos rather than giving your all to the practice.

The format used in most dojos originates in the traditional Japanese courtesy. Your sensei will have chosen the forms of etiquette which best express his or her ideals, perhaps using the forms passed on by his or her own teacher. Whatever the external forms may be, thoughtlessly mimicking them is an empty and meaningless gesture. As with the techniques, it is necessary to put your full spirit into the structure of etiquette, in order to give it life and meaning.

BALANCE

The balance between positive, strong (yang) and receptive, yielding (yin) is a vital one to practice in aikido. This balance exists within yourself, in relationship to your partner and as part of aikido techniques.

Balance of these attributes in aikido is not a precarious balance like walking a tightrope. It is a broad one. Balance is having a very strong, powerful side and at the same time a very sensitive, receptive side. True balance has unlimited amounts of both, and can call upon the appropriate amount of each, as dictated by the circumstances.

BALANCE WITHIN SELF

Within yourself the receptive side is the part that is sensitive and tranquil, so that it can receive information from the outside. The positive side is one of motion and committed action. Without receptivity, you will be moving blindly, like a bulldozer without a driver. With too much receptivity, you will be aware of a punch moving toward you, yet unable to move off the line of attack.

Two examples of this can be seen in the use of your hands and your eyes. A hand that is very positive is a fist. It is rigid and shaped to break something. A soft hand, one with which you would stroke a baby, is receptive, delicate. The open hand we use in aikido is both positive and receptive. It has extension and strength without being rigid. It is flexible and sensitive without being limp.

The eyes are also both positive and receptive. They are designed to take in information and to focus our attention and spirit. Seeing is the receptive aspect. Don't stare at any one part of your attacker or your vision will become narrow and fixated. Instead, open your eyes and let what you see come to you. But when you need to focus your attention and spirit, narrow your vision slightly and let your eyes be like a spotlight.

BALANCE WHILE TRAINING

As in all things in life, there is a bracket where learning happens best. This is where there is the perfect amount of stimulus. Too little, and our attention wanders and we lose interest. Too much, and we are overwhelmed. In aikido, it is especially important to maintain this balance; if practice becomes too vigorous for our partner's ability level, the likelihood of injury becomes very high and his fear becomes great enough to stop him from learning. Yet we must always train in a way that is challenging and appropriate.

Regardless of whether partners are of the same level of experience, or one person new and the other more senior, there exists a level of training that is both stimulating and joyful for both. Aikido is not a competitive sport. The purpose of training is not to butt egos with someone, but to learn to blend, with a mental attack as well as a physical one.

Training can at times be rigorous, even severe, but it should never be brutal.

Training in aikido gives a person great power, both physical and mental. With that power goes a grave responsibility to use it with love and compassion, to use it for learning and teaching, never for domination over another person.

BALANCE WITHIN A TECHNIQUE

A technique in taijutsu can be divided into three parts: attack/blend, transition, and completion.

In the first step, "uke" (attacker) attacks. He is the positive aspect and it is "nage's" (defender) job to be receptive and move in a way that aligns his body and spirit in the same direction as the attack. Once he merges, there is a moment where the energy dissipates from the attack. In this moment, nage takes the lead and becomes the positive aspect. Uke becomes receptive, losing his balance. Nage completes this cycle with a throw or pin. Uke, being receptive, absorbs the power in the throw with an "ukemi"—a controlled fall.

This scenario holds basically true for all practices, although the timing of the cycle alters considerably from technique to technique. Often the blend is exaggerated for practice. At other times, the middle section happens so quickly as to seem almost not there. It is a good practice to study a technique and find the points where uke is strong and nage is soft, where these roles begin to shift, and where they are fully reversed. What is important is to maintain the balance of positive and receptive between partners within the technique.

Aikido covers a wide range of practices. Some are quite sharp in their execution while others are very gentle. The balance must be maintained in each of these. In a hard style of training, you must have a spirit of loving protection for your partner. In a soft practice, don't be lulled into complacency by the soft outward appearance of the training. You must maintain a vigilant spirit at all times.

TOOLS FOR TRAINING

BLENDING/HARMONY

The first Japanese character in the name aikido is "ai," meaning harmony. Without harmony as a core principle in all techniques, aikido becomes simply a matter of being stronger than or faster than an opponent.

Harmony is a state where people and ideas are working in alignment. That harmony is broken at the moment someone attacks. It is our job to restore harmony, and the first step in doing so is to blend. A blend is a motion that acknowledges the existence of the attack and moves in a way that doesn't oppose it. The more we resist the attack, the stronger we make it. By blending, we dissipate the force of the attack and harness our power and that of the attacker.

In blending, we are not merely acquiescing and being overrun by the incoming force. It takes great balance and confidence to blend with a severe attack. We move, sometimes off the line of the attack, sometimes circularly, and sometimes through the middle of it.

KAMAE/HANMI/STANCE

In truth there are no "stances" in aikido. In freestyle there is a continual motion not limited by rigid poses. However, the process of learning aikido techniques and the principles behind them require clear static forms that give you first-hand experience of the fundamental principles being practiced.

The basic stance or "kamae" in aikido is called a "hanmi." A left hanmi is formed by placing your left foot forward and your right foot behind it, turned outward 90 degrees to the right. If you brought your feet together they would form a "T." Your knees are slightly bent, weight is evenly distributed between the feet. If you are relaxed, your left hip will be rotated slightly forward. This stance puts your whole body into the shape of a triangle.

A triangular stance is a stable yet flexible base to move from. You can quickly move to the left, right, front, or back. From this kamae you can even stay on the line of the attack, making your body like the prow of a ship. When an attack comes in, it is vectored around you. (See irimi-nage variations.)

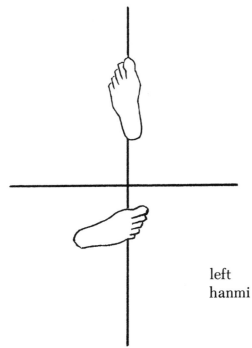

left
hanmi

MA-AI/HARMONIOUS DISTANCE

OMOTE/URA

Most techniques begin with "ma-ai" (harmonious distance) between the partners. From ma-ai it takes uke one committed step to reach nage with a strike or grab. Too close, and uke can hit without a step. If uke is this close, nage should already be in motion. The exception to this rule is when practicing static techniques from an attack such as a wrist hold or shoulder grasp. Even when practicing a static practice like this, have your body and spirit alive and ready to move. Simply wait until uke has a firm grip before you begin the technique.

It is important to become acutely aware of the ideal distance between you and your partner. It changes if he is taller or shorter or has a weapon in his hand, and you need to learn to intuitively adapt your stance and distance to changing circumstances.

Many basic techniques have two directions for their execution. "Omote-waza," also known as "irimi," is the entering, direct version of a technique. The same technique done with a turn is known as "ura-waza" or "tenkan."

Most omote-waza techniques begin by moving decisively toward and across the front of uke. This takes a deep step, and must be done in a committed move with the whole body and spirit, not just the arms. Entering techniques have a sharp, direct motion and spirit to them.

Ura-waza techniques are more absorbent in nature. They usually involve doing the technique while turning, bringing uke around nage's body in a spiralling movement.

The basic distinction between omote and ura exists in order to clearly learn the principles of entering and turning. At later stages of training, there is no formal omote-waza or ura-waza. At that point you will have internalized these principles and have the ability to enter or turn your body in an amount appropriate for that moment.

TAI-NO-HENKO

Tai-no-henko is a practice of blending, absorbing the power of someone's attack. It is also the basic structure of all ura-waza techniques. It should be practiced daily.

Uke is holding your right hand with her left. Your shoulder should be down and relaxed, your hand should be open and alive with spirit.

Shift your weight forward and turn your hips. Your hand must be in front of your center. Do not let it drag behind.

Step with your right foot until it meets her left, "toe-to-toe." Curl your own fingers until they are pointing to your center.

Step around with your left foot until you are standing in a right hanmi, facing the same direction as uke, with your hands extended directly out from your center.

NOTEBOOK

too shallow

too deep

If you enter too deeply with your initial step, you will push against uke's power. If your step is too shallow, your hand will drag behind you as you turn. Step-

ping toe-to-toe makes your body turn in relation to uke as a door turns on its hinges.

wrong   *right*

Keep your hands in front of your center. If you leave your hand in front of uke, you will develop the habit of leaving it behind you during the execution of all ura-waza techniques. Also, you should consider her attack to be not just a grasp, but possibly a strike with a hand or sword. Your hands and center must move together.

Tai-no-henko should also be done in motion, "ki-no-nagare." Do the exact same moves as in the basic technique, but begin moving before uke can grasp hold. Perform this practice at a walking pace so that nage can clearly feel when he is blending with uke's attack and when he is not.

CENTERING RELAXATION

When your body and mind are relaxed yet alert and ready to move, you are centered. In this state you are no less aware than normal of fear, anger, or physical sensations such as being hit or bumped. Actually you are more aware of them, because being centered increases your sensitivity. But in this state you are not at the mercy of emotions and physical disturbances. It is as though you were at the eye of a storm. The winds and rain are raging on all sides, yet it is quiet and peaceful where you stand.

To begin developing this quality of inner peace, spend a few minutes before class sitting straight and quiet. Focus your attention at your center/ hips and breathe slowly, deeply, and quietly.

When you can maintain this centeredness in the midst of turmoil, such as freestyle practice, a severe attack, or other difficult times, the beginnings of mastery are emerging. Mastery ultimately is not a challenge of winning over an opponent. As the Founder put it, "Winning means winning over the mind of discord within yourself."

EXTENSION/KOKYU

Extension is the motion of power emanating from the center of your body through your arms or other parts of your body. This extension is not simply pushing with the muscles of your arms, but uniting all the power in your body, legs, arms, mind, and spirit into a coordinated motion.

Extension has a number of aspects. There is, for example, the shape and motion of the arm and hand and body, and the aligning of energy to drive the body.

The hand and arm move in a spiral outward from the body. The hand is open and the shoulders are low and relaxed. The sensation is that water is flowing from the fire hydrant (your body) through the hose (arm), out the nozzle (hand). If the hose is kinked (arm overly bent) or the shoulder is tense, it stops the flow.

The water in the above analogy is "ki," universal energy. This energy is the subtle life force that is behind every state of being and motion. In Japanese language, the word ki is used to describe health (gen-ki), sickness (byo-ki) as well as aiki (harmonious spirit).

Learning to harness the inner powers of energy is accomplished through practices designed to develop a power called "kokyu-ryoku" (breath power). Kokyu (breath) ties the realm of energy to that of the body. Breath is like a needle

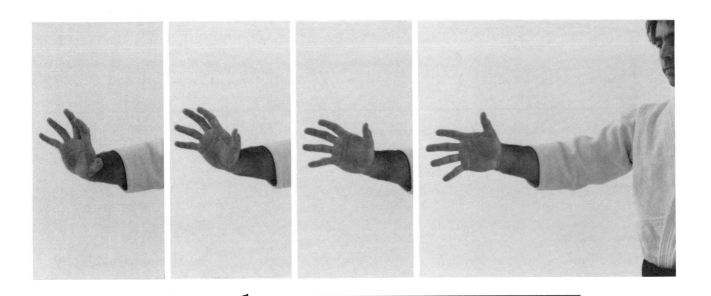

weaving the thread of energy through the fabric of the body. The movements and power of kokyu are used in all techniques in aikido. Aikido without kokyu would be a car without gasoline.

The two main practices for developing kokyu-ryoku are morote-dori kokyu-ho and kokyu-dosa. These simple techniques, practiced daily, teach the power of uniting your body, mind, and spirit.

MOROTE-DORI KOKYU-HO

Uke holds your right arm firmly with both of her hands. Keep your shoulders low, and your fingers open wide.

Lower your elbow, shoulder, hips and your spirit.

Step beside uke with your right foot. Turn your body counter-clockwise. Draw your left foot under you until you are standing in a left hanmi facing the same direction as uke. Both hands should be in front of you.

Keeping your right elbow extended out towards uke, raise your arms and step behind uke with your right foot.

Bring your arms down, lower your hips by bending your knees.

Shift towards uke, turn your arms and hips towards her. Don't look towards her.

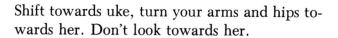

KOKYU-DOSA

Begin exhaling. Turn your hands in a spiral towards uke. His elbows will rise. Keep your elbows below the level of your hands.

BASIC

Seated before your partner, hold your hands out in front of you. Have your fingers open and filled with energy.

Turn your hands slightly palm-upward to connect the back of your hand to uke's arm. Inhale deeply into the center of your body.

Shift your body forward and slightly to the side, bringing uke over. Continue exhaling.

Turn on your knees until facing uke. Extend down, but do not push on him.

When uke changes his attack it is important to learn how to alter the technique to match his direction and force. For example, instead of holding from the side, uke might be holding nage's wrists from above or from below. He might be holding very tightly, pinning the hands down, or possibly holding the elbows. Appropriate variations exist for all of these, although only two of these will be demonstrated here. Remember, ninety percent of the time you should practice the basic version.

WRISTS HELD FROM ABOVE

Uke holds nage's wrists from above.

As you lift your arm to do the basic kokyu-dosa, arch your body back slightly drawing him toward you. Do not over-do this or he will fall over you.

Rotate your hands as shown and continue with the basic kokyu-dosa.

Rotate your hands as shown and continue with basic kokyu-dosa.

WRISTS HELD FROM BELOW

This is a common way for people to hold. If you try to enter straight in, your hand will ride over uke's shoulders.

Uke holds nage's wrists from below.

Place the back of your hands against uke's wrists and draw down and slightly out until uke is pulled slightly off balance.

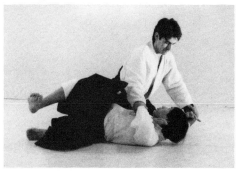

KEN JO TAIJUTSU RIAI

Aikido is known mostly for "taijutsu," its throwing/pinning techniques. Equally important as taijutsu, however, is the practice of "aiki ken" (sword) and "aiki jo" (staff). Ken and jo teach aspects of aikido that are often more difficult to perceive while doing taijutsu practices. The principles of extension and focus, for example, become much clearer after practicing with a sword. Through the many sword practices, your ability to concentrate and move becomes blade-like in its sharpness.

The term used to describe the relationship between empty-handed practice and weapons practice is "ken, jo, taijutsu riai." The word "riai" means harmony of principles. Aikido is a way of movement that is consistent regardless of whether you are empty-handed or holding a ken or jo. For example, if

your hips would lower at a certain point in a taijutsu technique, something would be wrong if you raised them at that same point while doing the technique with a sword. Certain turns or extensions, which are often difficult in taijutsu, become quite clear while doing the similar motion with a sword in your hands. An example of using the ken to study a technique appears in the chapter on shiho-nage. Study this and apply your understanding to other practices.

A word of warning! Eventually, the feeling when you pick up a ken or jo is that your blood courses through it, that it is as much a part of you as your arm or leg. This will happen slowly and only with many years of practice. Even if you have been practicing taijutsu for many years, don't expect this feeling or understanding to develop immediately. Patiently begin practicing the basic "suburi."* With diligent practice, the synthesis of ken/jo/taijutsu will evolve naturally within your body.

* See *Traditional Aikido* Vol. I, SAITO

UKEMI

Ukemi translates "receive through the body." In aikido, uke—the one who does this receiving—is the person who plays the role of attacker in practice. First, he attacks nage—defender—with a strike or grab. Then, if nage successfully blends and does a throw, uke must move with the technique, receive it with his body, and fall in such a way as not to be injured. This is the initial form of ukemi, but there is a great deal more to it than meets the eye.

Ukemi is the actual vehicle through which you learn aikido. What you receive through your body as uke is not the losing end of someone else's execution of an aikido technique. You receive the essence of aikido itself. Bit by bit, your body and senses are learning the movement and energy of the technique as it is being done to you. You are learning what feels strong and right, and what does not. Aikido is thus transmitted directly from body to body.

It is important, therefore, to pay strict attention to both the form and the spirit of ukemi. Practice falls until they are second nature. The way you fall affects your perceptions of aikido. If you fall with a great amount of fear or tension, then your attention will be on escaping pain or injury. When you become nage, your concept of the technique will be clouded by the tension you had while learning it as uke. When ukemi becomes natural, then your focus can be on the technique.

Aikido practice is unique in that instead of both partners attacking and competing for the upper hand in an encounter, one partner is designated attacker, the other, defender. Uke is offering himself as attacker in the practice. This must be done with full sincerity.

During class, the form for practice is usually set up by the sensei. Hence, both uke and nage know in advance what the form will be. The challenge is to give an honest attack not altered by the knowledge of what nage will probably do. An honest punch to the chest is just that: a punch to the chest. A punch to the chest should hit nage in the chest if he stands still, and miss if he gets off the line of attack. It's neither helpful to your partner nor is it a good practice to shy away and miss when nage does not get off the line. Nor is it good training to redirect the strike in the direction nage is going in order to make it harder on him. Pretend you don't know what technique he is going to do, and simply give a solid, straight, balanced punch.

These rules are for basic practice. More advanced practices such as freestyle practice or "kaeshi-waza" (countering techniques) demand that uke be freer in his attack.

This must be done at a level appropriate to both your and your partner's ability. A beginner deserves the same integrity in an attack as an advanced student. The only difference is the speed and power with which it is done. A beginner should be hit if he stays on the line, just more slowly than a black belt. Conversely, your attack should be at the speed and power of your ability to fall. If you can safely fall at no

more than seven mph, don't attack at seventy mph.

Understand, it's not as if the attacker is doing a strike so that nage can practice an aikido technique on uke. Both are still doing aikido. Uke is practicing a strong, committed, positive beginning; nage is being receptive and blending with the attack. As nage begins to take control, to become the positive aspect of the practice, uke balances the situation and becomes yielding, receptive, taking a fall. Ukemi is therefore a practice in preserving balance, not in losing it.

An important aikido training method involves offering resistance to your partner. *This should not be done by beginners.* It is a practice of stressing the technique to discover weak, ineffective areas and requires nage to practice with his whole body and spirit. It takes great sensitivity, not strength, to do this so that it enhances the practice. Too much, and it's a battle of wills; too little, and it isn't stimulating. This practice must also be done in the purest of spirits, as a gift. All too easily, it becomes an ego game. This is quite

destructive and should be avoided. Done in the correct manner, at the right time, in the purest of spirits, this intensified style of practice can be quite valuable.

Ukemi is also an opportunity to see clearly in practice the different ways we react to fear, pressure, and pain. To take safe, fluid falls requires you to be completely aware of the motion and relaxed enough to adapt your body to it and absorb the power of the throw. Fear and pain cause you to tighten up, to withdraw when it is time to be 100-percent committed to the motion that is happening in that moment.

It is through the practice of ukemi that the relationship between emotion and body motion can be perceived, an inner understanding of the workings of the technique felt, and both turned into knowledge within the body.

TECHNIQUES

PROGRESSION OF PRACTICE

There are five techniques presented in this book. Ikkyo, irimi-nage, shiho-nage, koshi-nage and kokyu-nage. Though there are literally hundreds of techniques and thousands of variations that could be covered, this book is not meant to be a comprehensive encyclopedia of aikido. Instead, its intention is to delve deeply into a few techniques, study their form, their spirit, their beginnings, and their evolution as we progress.

One of the most important lessons I've learned while both training and teaching is something that might seem obvious: that it is practice of the techniques of aikido that teaches aikido to us. We discover the true aiki principles within ourselves while practicing. When the instructor is demonstrating and discussing harmony and blending, we are impressed with his ability, and possibly understand the concept intellectually, but it is not until we directly experience moving in accord with an attacker that we truly have discovered the concrete principle of harmony. The teacher's role is therefore to set up the circumstances and environment in which the student can discover aikido within himself.

Each of the techniques presented here teaches some aspect of aikido clearly. Ikkyo teaches connection, irimi-nage guides our understanding of entering and commitment in motion. But each aspect discovered in each technique also exists to some extent in all techniques. It is the student's job to take these lessons and apply them to all his aikido training.

Each technique will be divided into three levels of training: its basic/static form, its more fluid versions, and variations that are derived from the basic technique. These stages exist for training in all the arts. For a musician, the first level would be to play a melody, the second to add some harmony to the original melody, and the third to play variations on the theme.

KIHON WAZA
STATIC BASIC TECHNIQUE

Basic techniques are where we study the mechanics or the form of a technique, and it is to the basics that we must return time and time again to check ourselves and to correct our understanding of that part of aikido upon which we base more advanced aspects of the art. The techniques must be practiced over and over again, while we study the movement of the feet, hands, center, and the relationship with uke. The practice must be slow, deliberate, and repeated until the form and principles being practiced become second nature.

These basic techniques, when done correctly, call all parts of your body and spirit to task so that aikido is learn-ed with your whole being. Your hands, feet, hips, eyes—every atom in your body—must be involved. Even the parts of your body that seem not to be needed, such as a hand that is not being used, must be filled with spirit and feel fully involved. Any part that is not participating will detract from the whole.

These basics are therefore not only the foundation of the techniques, but also the instruments through which we discover and practice the principles of centering, extending, blending. Basic technique is not just an important step for beginners, it is imperative that advanced students continually reinforce this basic foundation as part of their daily practice.

KI NO NAGARE
FLOWING PRACTICE

Fluid training is the step after basics. The different parts of the technique are put together into a whole. The practice is looked at as a unit, as a single movement, studying the motion and the timing of the technique.

Do the techniques slowly at first. Then increase the speed and power as you practice. At first, the motions will have corners where the parts were put together. Do not rush or avoid areas that are rough. With practice, the corners will round out and the technique will be done smoothly.

Be careful not to lose the power and clarity of the basic technique. It is not a trade-off between power on one hand and timing and smoothness on the other. Timing and smoothness are added to the form of the technique, not substituted for it. So begin this stage slowly, adding just a little motion to the technique at a time. If the technique begins to falter, slow down, regain a strong footing in the basic form, and then start again with the fluid practice.

Fluid does not necessarily mean soft. It means that you begin your motion of blending with uke before he arrives with his attack, and also, that the execution of the technique be done in a continual motion. The training can be hard or soft, but in either case, it must be filled with commitment and spirit.

TAKE-MUSU AIKI OYO-WAZA/VARIATIONS

Take-Musu Aiki is the term O'Sensei used to describe the level of aikido that develops after many years of training in basic through advanced practices of taijutsu, ken and jo. The idea is that, after years of rigorous training, when the principles of aiki are thoroughly a part of you, creativity begins to flow through the well-honed tool of your body and mind, allowing for the discovery of new techniques and ways of moving.

I use this term, Take-Musu Aiki, for lack of a better one, to describe the more advanced levels of aikido where rigid form begins to disappear and a more spontaneous way of movement takes its place.

This level is much more than just the unhampered "creativity" which is abundant in all of us. It is the level of mastery where our body becomes sufficiently tuned through training to be capable of expressing creativity in aikido. This is the stage, for a musician, where technique and hearing and understanding of musical theory are sufficient to express inner musical ideas. This ability comes slowly. The feeling is not so much *doing* a technique as *becoming* the technique. This is not a stage you can practice. When your body and mind are trained sufficiently, it will begin to happen all by itself and can neither be forced nor hindered.

In the chapters that follow, the techniques in the advanced section will not be demonstrations of "Take-Musu Aiki," for there is no way to adequately demonstrate that spontaneity in a book. They will be "oyo-waza," more advanced variations and expressions of the technique that will offer some guidance toward understanding aikido more fully.

In studying the techniques, understand that these are far from all the attributes the techniques express and far from all the variations that exist. There are thousands of variations that exist and undoubtedly will be practiced at some time in the course of your training.

一

教 KATATE DORI

IKKYO

Traditionally, ikkyo is the first technique studied in aikido, hence its very name, "first teaching." Its nickname, given by some of the old-timers, "lifetime technique," hints at the importance of continuous training in this technique, for it holds many of the secrets of aikido within it, and it only gives up these secrets slowly over a period of many years of study.

Though outwardly a simple technique, the practice of ikkyo teaches some of aikido's primary and important principles. Ikkyo is also the basis for the more complex techniques of nikkyo, sankyo, and yonkyo.

Ikkyo is a technique of connection. The first step in learning connection is learning the skill of how to hold. Grasp by molding your hand around your partner's hand or arm. Hold mainly with the little finger, ring finger and thumb. The other fingers hold, but less firmly. This grip leaves no air space between your palm and his hand or arm.

The next connection is that of your hands with your own body. The hands are an extension of the body and they must move as one with it, neither ahead nor behind. As you turn your body and bring uke's arm down and around, it is imperative to keep both your hands in front of your body and not let them drag behind you. You must be in harmony with yourself before you can even begin to harmonize with another person.

BASIC FORM

OMOTE-WAZA

Stand in a right hanmi. Uke grabs your right wrist with his left. Open your fingers wide and extend your spirit out through them. Your right hand and your right foot move together, well off to the right side. Your left foot adjusts to form a left hanmi facing uke. Your left hand does a strike towards his face.

Keeping your attention on uke, your outside hand extended, move your inside hand down to meet uke's hand. Grasp uke's hand.

Raise both of your hands together, and begin entering deeply towards uke with your left foot.

Your right hand frees itself from his grip and grasps uke's elbow from below. Extend his elbow towards his head. Shift your weight forward towards him. This should cause him to lose his balance.

Keeping you hands directly in front of you, turn your hips and bring uke's arm down in a spiral until uke completely loses his balance.

Step deeply towards your partner with your right foot. Keep both hands extended. Don't change your grip while pinning his shoulder to the mat. Your hand should still be holding his elbow.

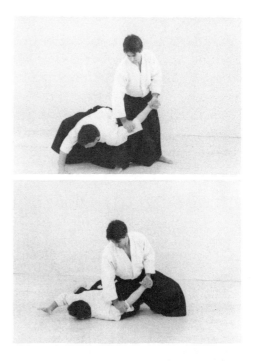

Once uke's shoulder is firmly pinned to the mat, place your inside knee in his armpit. Then, bring his arm down so that it is pinned 90 degrees to his body and your left knee is firmly touching his arm. Stretch his arm away from his body and pin it down.

URA-WAZA

As in ikkyo omote-waza, the emphasis in ikkyo ura-waza is on connection with your partner. It is much easier to connect while moving towards your partner and it is more difficult while rotating away. Your tie with uke must be complete before turning. It is easy to lose contact with him and end up tugging on his arm.

Step off the line with your left foot and hand at the same time, just as you do in omote-waza. Do a strike with your free hand.

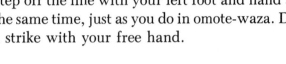

Keeping your focus on your partner, slide the hand that did the strike down his arm and grasp the back of his hand.

Raise both of your hands up towards his head. Step forward with your left foot so that it is right in front of his forward foot (toe-to-toe); simultaneously grasp his elbow from below.

Continue the spiral until his shoulder is firmly pinned to the ground. Bring your body beside him just as in omote-waza.

Keep an extension through his elbow. As you sweep your right foot behind uke, bring your right hand down and around your body as though it were chasing your right leg. Simultaneously extend through your left hand to bring his arm down and around your body in a spiral.

Detail of elbow grip.

Detail of hand hold.

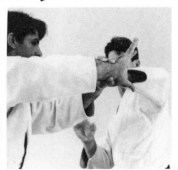

When moving the hand that did an "atemi" (strike) down to grasp his hand, do not look at either hand. Your attention must not wander from your partner or you will become vulnerable.

Both hands are part of the extension. Don't pull up with the hand that is holding his hand.

wrong

 right

Ura-waza:
As you enter toe-to-toe and begin the spiral, be careful to not enter so deeply that your partner falls backwards as in omote-waza. If you do this, you will have to drag him around. Instead, extend through his elbow just enough to make him lose his balance slightly.

If you lose your extension and raise your elbow, you will not be able to draw uke around or down.

wrong

right

A common error in ura-waza is to lose sight of the direction in which you are moving and to look back at your partner. Looking back will stop your spiraling extension and create a split between your hands, center, head and spirit. They must all move around and down as a single unit.

There is a tendency to step forward with your outside foot as uke nears the ground. Uke will be able to easily take his hand away. If he is on your right side, keep your right foot forward until his shoulder is firmly on the ground.

wrong

When pinning, uke's arm should be at a right angle to his body. At too shallow an angle, the pin will have no effect. If the angle is too great, it is painful but he can easily withdraw his hand from you.

right

too high

KI-NO-NAGARE

OMOTE-WAZA

In the next stage in ikkyo training, connection progresses from a hold at the hands to one that is from center to center. The hands act as wires to transmit that connection from your center to that of your partner.

Connection with a person is not a static state. It is always changing. Merge with the motion of his body, the motion of his hand, and the direction of his intent. To create and maintain this relationship with someone in motion, you must learn to be adaptable and flexible both physically and mentally.

The fundamental moves are almost identical for both omote and ura-waza. The moves are rounder and smoother than the basic technique.

Following the same path, begin with uke moving in to grab. As he nears you, move off the line as before so that uke can just barely reach your hand. Don't wait for him to attack; move in synch with his attack.

Don't try to be fast. Move with your partner, smoothly, without stops or breaks in the technique. To do this, practice executing the technique with a single prolonged exhalation.

URA-WAZA

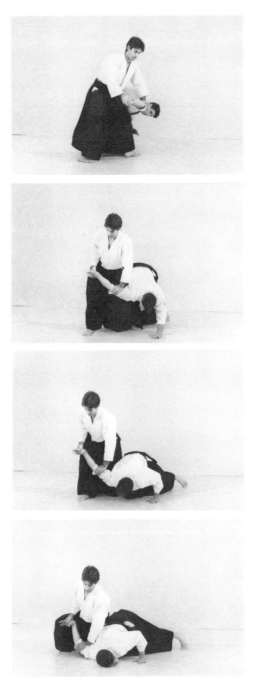

VARIATIONS

OMOTE-WAZA

Through extended practice, you will come to understand that the simple connection that at first was a practice of holding, then one of connecting well with yourself, then one of connecting center to center, develops into a deep understanding of the universal bond of which we are all a part.

As uke enters to grab your hand, take a large step backwards with your right foot. Leave your hand in front of you, just enough so that he can almost get a hold. Keep your spirit sharply focussed on uke, not on his hand.

Grasp from above as before. Draw your partner down off balance then up in a big arc. This must be done in one smooth move.

Enter into omote-waza or turn into ura-waza or choose a direction somewhere between the two, if appropriate.

VARIATIONS

URA-WAZA

NIKKYO URA-WAZA

Nikkyo is an excellent example of the more complex variations on the principles of connection learned from the practice of ikkyo.

Begin the technique with the same movement off the line done in the basic katate-dori ikkyo ura-waza.

Instead of grasping his elbow, your right hand holds his wrist and draws his hand into the soft spot located next to your right shoulder and just below the collar-bone. Change from a left hanmi into a right hanmi facing him. Pull in with both of your hands so that his elbow is bent.

Continue to draw in and at the same time bend your knees and bow. The pressure at his wrist will cause him to drop close to your feet.

Sit on your heels up on your toes with your right knee next to his arm-pit and your left knee near his head. Hold your left shoulder with your right hand, hold his arm against your body with your left. Keep his arm straight and shift your weight over his head and down to pin.

Extend your right arm beneath his left elbow and extend around and down as shown. Continue the nikkyo pressure on his wrist.

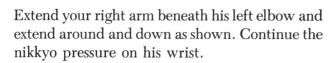

四方投げ

KATATE DORI
SHIHO-NAGE

Shiho-nage, "four direction throw," is a practice of expanding conscious-ness. Beginning with katate-dori, wrist grab, you can move directly to any one of the four directions: front, back, left, or right. Since you can move to any of those directions, you can then move between those points for eight sides, between those angles for 16 directions, and so on.

Shiho-nage therefore is the practice of "infinite mobility"—being able to move with ease from any direction to any other direction.

Initially, this is a practice of smoothly moving the feet and hips from one direction to another. This soon translates into being able to extend and be aware to the front, back, left, and right with ease. When the difference between directions disappears, you move more like the radiance of the sun, emanating equally in all directions.

BASIC FORM

OMOTE-WAZA

Raise both hands together. The right hand is open and should be rotating in a spiral. Your right elbow should be under your partner's elbow, extending up into it. Begin to twist your hips.

Open your fingers wide. Step with your forward foot to the outside and slightly forward. Draw the back foot up and turn your body until you are in a left hanmi with your hand directly in front of you. You should be standing about 90 degrees to your partner. Hold your partner's hand from above your left hand. (See detail of grip in notebook.)

Step forward and in a circle with your back foot. Shift your hips under your arm. Keep your partner's arm stretched.

Rotate your body all the way around behind your partner. Your hands should be slightly behind your partner's shoulder, and directly in front of your head. You need to be in a solid stance or you will wobble.

Cut down in a spiral around you. Keep your hands in front of you. As your partner falls, sweep your right foot backwards until you are in a hanmi, 45 degrees to his body.

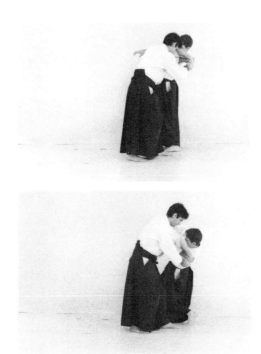

URA-WAZA

Rotate your elbow forward and underneath your partner's elbow in a kokyu motion. Hold his hand with the other hand as shown. Step deeply behind your partner with your back foot. If this step is shallow, you won't be able to turn your hips enough. At this point you will be facing the same direction as your partner.

Shift your forward foot ahead until your toes align with your partner's forward foot. Begin to rotate your hand in a spiral.

Extend your hands up and away from your partner. Turn your body 180 degrees until facing completely behind your partner's back. Your hands should be aligned with your head.

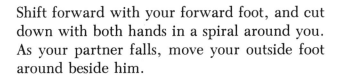

Shift forward with your forward foot, and cut down with both hands in a spiral around you. As your partner falls, move your outside foot around beside him.

Detail of grasp in omote-waza.

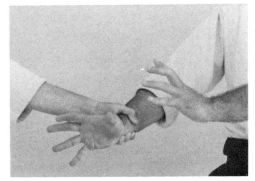

Detail of grasp in ura-waza.

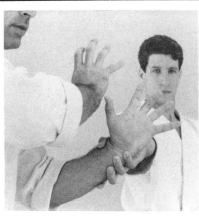
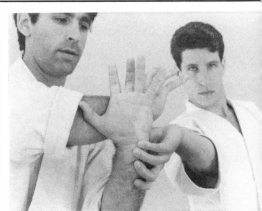

It's vital to get his hand, along with your hands and hips, completely behind his shoulder. In order to do this, your feet must move sufficiently to face the new direction. If you don't step around enough, you will have to twist your hips painfully or reach with your hands away from your own center.

Be careful not to turn so far around that your back foot slides forward. Your inside hand and foot must remain forward/positive. If the back foot moves beyond the front foot, then the side close to your partner becomes receptive and he can easily pull his hand away.

wrong

wrong

wrong

right

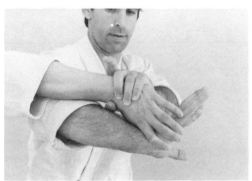

Keep your hands in front of your body. It is easy to let them drag behind. Special care should be taken just before the throw to keep them in front of your head.

You should be standing approximately 45 degrees out from uke. If you stand over his head, he can pull you over or strike you.

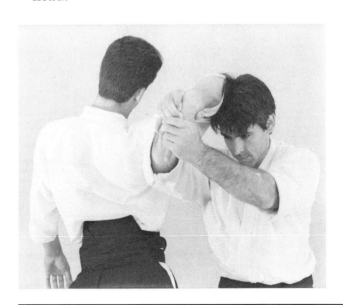

KI-NO-NAGARE

Ki-no-nagare translates as "flowing energy," and that's exactly how nage merges with uke's attack, like two rivers flowing together. Visualize the whole motion before your partner moves. Extend your spirit out in all directions as you turn.

The movements of ura-waza and omote-waza are the same as the basic form. Begin moving before your partner arrives so that at the moment of contact you are moving at the same speed as your partner's attack. This allows you to merge smoothly without clashing. Move too slowly and you will collide; too fast, and you will separate.

OMOTE-WAZA

URA-WAZA

KEN/TAIJUTSU RIAI RELATIONSHIP OF TAIJUTSU AND SWORD

The moves of shiho-nage and the moves of the sword are almost the same. The feelings from one translate into the other. If you are having trouble with shiho-nage, study the similar moves using a bokken, then apply that feeling to shiho-nage.

One of the important aspects to note is that when you are cutting with a sword, you are cutting to his center, not towards his sword. In tai-jutsu, the feeling is also of doing the technique towards his center, not just his arm.

UKE AND NAGE HOLDING SWORDS

NAGE HOLDING SWORD
UKE GRABS BOTH HANDS

VARIATIONS

There is no front, no back, no left, no right. Conscious in all directions, move through shiho-nage.

You can begin shiho-nage by stepping back with your left foot instead of off the line. You must not pause after stepping back, nor turn your back on uke. Even while stepping backward, maintain a positive extension toward uke.

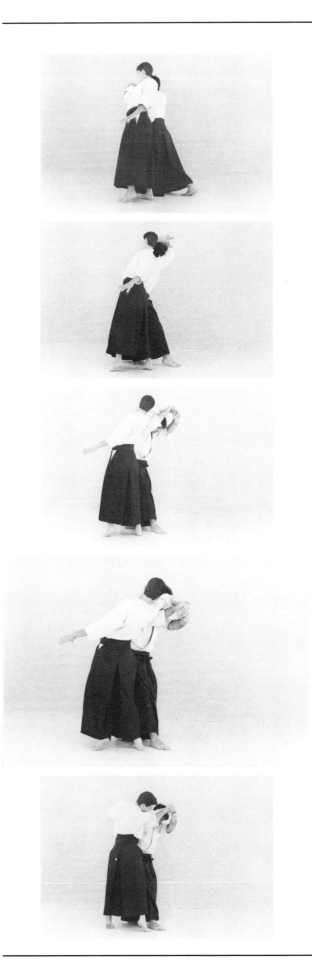

腰投げ

RYOTE DORI
KOSHI-NAGE

Koshi-nage, like ikkyo, is a teaching in connection. The connection in koshi-nage is one that is transmitted not through the arms but directly from body to body. As there is no space between water and the rock over which it flows, there is no space between nage's and uke's bodies. This bond permeates aikido; hip to hip, body close to body. Regular training in koshi-nage develops our understanding of this relationship, builds strength in our hips, and enables us to transfer that power and understanding to other techniques.

There are two fundamental types of koshi-nage: one in which you enter by moving your head under uke's arm, and another in which you rotate your hips beneath him.

HEAD UNDER

Your right foot steps forward directly between uke's feet. At the same time, extend down with your right hand towards his right knee. Your left hand comes to the inside of uke's hand, extends up and holds his wrist.

Lower your weight towards uke until your hips are below his center of gravity. Extend your left hand, stretching him up over your body, and "sight" up along your arm. Make sure his hips are firmly engaged with the small of your back.

Extend your hand down beneath your body, twist your hips, and completely shift your weight onto your left foot. This will rotate uke around your body into a fall.

Shift your weight towards your left foot, maintaining the extension with your left arm.

HIPS UNDER

Extend his arms upward. Step in front of uke with your right foot.

Uke stands in a left hanmi. Step off the line to the right with your right foot. Draw your left foot up until your feet are in a left hanmi facing 90 degrees to your partner. Both hands make a counterclockwise circle and hold uke's wrists.

Lower your hips as you turn to the left so that your left foot steps between uke's feet. Bending your knees, shift towards uke until your hips connect with uke's body below his center of gravity. Keep uke stretched over your body. Sight up along your own arms.

Twist your hips, shifting your weight towards your right foot, and extend uke's arms around and down for the throw.

HIPS UNDER
DIRECT ENTRANCE

This version of koshi-nage is identical to the previous form except that instead of stepping off the line and then into koshi-nage, you enter directly in.

Lift uke's hands, and step between uke's feet with your right foot. Hold his hands as shown in the previous koshi-nage.

Turn counter-clockwise, step between uke's feet with your left foot, lowering your hips. Stretch his arms up and forward and bind him to your hips below his center of gravity.

Shift your weight onto your forward foot and roll him over you as in the previous koshi-nage.

You can grip uke's wrists either from above or from below as shown.

Your body and uke's body should be at 90 degrees to each other in the shape of a cross when you load him onto your hips. Connect your hips to his below his center of gravity. The point of connection should be more towards your forward hip. Practicing this will make you quite flexible in the hip. Bend the knee that is close to uke and look up along your own arm. If you look down it will move your hip away from him.

If you extend uke's arms over your hips, he will load on your hips. If you bring his hands over your upper body, he will ride up over your back or shoulders, making him seem very heavy. Also, if he is up too high, he can easily reach around your neck as you throw.

wrong

right

You must keep uke extended up and off balance in the direction of the throw. Sight up your extended arm towards the ceiling to assure that you are doing that. Don't pull down on his arm before you throw, as it will bind his upper body to you, making it difficult to throw.

wrong

right

wrong

As you throw, continue to shift forward to keep him off balance forward until your weight is mostly on your front foot. If you leave your weight back, he might land on your front leg.

When you first practice koshi-nage it will feel more as if you are lifting uke's weight up. As you improve your understanding of the angles of the throw, hip placement, and proper spirit, uke will feel very light. Done properly, koshi-nage can easily be done by someone very small to someone much heavier.

KI-NO-NAGARE

Align your motion so that at the moment of contact with uke, you are moving at the same speed and direction he is. Blend body and spirit, and you will be moving through space together, in harmony.

The form of the fluid style of koshi-nage is the same as in the static version. Begin moving at the same time and speed as he does so that your hips meet smoothly. Practice doing this without lifting uke's weight. Instead, guide his incoming grab upwards as you lower your body underneath his.

HEAD UNDER

HIPS UNDER

HIPS UNDER
DIRECT ENTRANCE

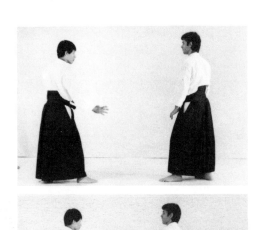

VARIATIONS

BLEND BACK
INTO KOSHI-NAGE

There is unity in all of existence. Our choice is whether to see it and move from that knowledge. The rock and the water are both part of the river. The river doesn't call the rock an attacker. The rock is there, and the river flows around it in harmony. When we view uke as an opponent, we have already set into motion opposition and conflict. See him as part of the universe, just as you are, and move with him, already in harmony.

Blend deeply back, absorbing his incoming force. Guide him up and continue his outward extension, lowering your hips beneath him. Do koshinage as before.

KOSHI-NAGE KOKYU-NAGE RELATIONSHIP

Almost all koshi-nage's can easily become kokyu-nage techniques. This is done by placing your hips beside your partner's instead of underneath.

Begin with any of the basic koshi-nage techniques shown. While stretching his arms forward, step forward and toward him while pushing the side of your hip into his hip. This will cause him to lose his balance and fall.

OFF THE LINE OF ATTACK INTO KOKYU-NAGE

DIRECT BLEND INTO KOKYU-NAGE

BLEND BACK INTO KOKYU-NAGE

呼吸投げ

KATATE DORI
KOKYU-NAGE

Kokyu translates as "breath" in Japanese. The word "kokyu-nage" means, therefore, "breath throw." In aikido however, kokyu means much more than simple inhalation and exhalation.

Energy, "ki" in Japanese, is a subtle vibration within the body and outside the body. It is this life force that is behind all awareness and motion. Ki/energy is subtle and often hard to feel, but the effect of harnessing it in unity with physical motion is spectacular in the power it calls forth. Simply to perceive this subtle vibration requires an inner quiet, such as is practiced during meditation. Aikido is often called a meditation in motion because of the heightened awareness that comes from training.

Bringing the body, mind, and ki/energy into a state of complete unity is the function of kokyu. Breath is the thread that links intentions, mind, and spirit with the motions of the body and brings them into the world as one.

BASIC FORM

Uke begins by grasping your left hand with his right. Keeping your shoulder low, turn your left hand towards your own center. Step beside your partner with your left foot, and turn to face the same direction he is facing. Both of your hands should be in front of you.

Lower your hips by bending your knees. Begin extending your arm up under his chin and then stand up.

Step deeply behind your partner with your left foot, shifting your weight and twisting your hips and arms towards him.

As he falls, bend your knees and lower your arms. Both of your hands should be extended, palms up, in front of your center.

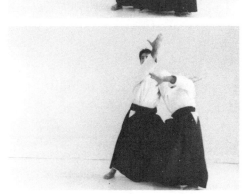

wrong   *right*   *wrong*

Don't look at your partner while throwing. If you look at your partner while entering, your hands will lag behind you and lose power, and uke will be able to step back and escape. It will also become difficult to get your hip close to him.

The purpose of the step behind uke is to make a solid connection at the hips (see koshi-nage). If you don't step deeply enough behind uke, then your arm will be running directly into his power. Get close so that your arm will rotate around uke without clashing against his body. Your hips then will supply all the power for the technique.

detail of nage's arm rotating around uke ⟶

Both hands move together. If your left hand moves to the left and your right hand to the right, your hips will jut forward, causing you to lose your balance. If you are turning counterclockwise, your left hand extends left, as does your right hand. Your hips, located between both hands, will then be stable and empower the throw. The second hand can easily do an atemi (strike).

KI-NO-NAGARE

When performing this technique fluidly, remember to preserve the basic structure. Move smoothly; don't rush and leave out important parts of the form. Speed and power will come naturally only when you are doing this correctly.

Ki-no-nagare motions are often circular; if you rush to move from point "a" on a circle to point "b," your linear movement will cut off part of the circle, making a rough spot or corner in execution of the technique.

VARIATIONS

DIRECT ENTRANCE

Reduce the size of each motion of the basic practice without leaving any blend, extension, or hip turn out. This entrance must be done in a piercing, committed motion and spirit.

As uke steps towards you to grasp your hand, step forward with your left foot. At the same time extend your left hand toward uke, spiralling it from a palm down to a palm up position.

EMPHASIZING THE SECOND HAND

The right hand could be a strike as it moves towards uke's abdomen. In this case, grab hold of his belt and draw his hips forward while extending upward with your left arm.

Turn your left hand over and place the palm of your hand on his chin. Extend over and down. Practice this carefully, so as not to injure uke.

KOKYU-NAGE
INTO A PIN

As uke comes to grasp your left hand, begin blending as in the basic form.

Grasp his incoming hand from the top with your right hand. Step completely around with your right foot as in tai-no-henko. Bar his right arm across your chest by drawing your right hand back around your body; simultaneously extend up into his chin with your left elbow.

After he is pinned to your body, start slipping him downward. Turn your left hand over and grasp his neck.

Lower yourself onto your right knee, and firmly pin his arm onto your left leg.

KOKYU-NAGE INTO IRIMI-NAGE

Aikido is a practice in both physical and mental flexibility. If the attack alters or if for some reason it is not appropriate to continue with a technique, you can easily slip into another. This adaptability is important for free style training, where a rigid mentality would make it difficult to deal rapidly with many attackers. However, it is not a good way to practice basic techniques, since this style of training avoids areas of difficulty which you would thus miss the opportunity to discover and study.

ARM SLIPS OFF UKE'S CHIN

Begin kokyu-nage as in the basic motion.

As your elbow nears his chin, it slips off and over his shoulder.

Shift your whole body in beside him. Hold his
hand with your left hand. Position your right
shoulder under his right arm. Move your own
head close to him.

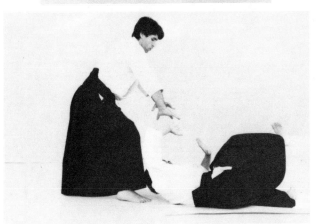

Extend your right arm as in irimi-nage and step
in behind him with your right foot.

入身投げ

SHOMEN UCHI
IRIMI-NAGE

As uke begins to strike, we have already entered through her to her center. Just as a sword strike cuts without hesitation or doubt, enter behind your partner. Irimi-nage cuts through to the heart of aikido. It teaches a gentle compassion and at the same time has the razor-sharp spirit of the sword.

You must practice irimi-nage often, but be prepared for many years of being both baffled and excited by this technique. Irimi nage is known as "the twenty-year technique." Training in irimi-nage is like threading a needle. You cannot force it. When the thread is lined up with the eye of the needle, it will thread with ease.

BASIC FORM

Keeping your extension, step in deep with your right foot. At this point you want to be standing behind uke in the same hanmi. Keep her forward hand extended out, hold her collar.

Both partners begin standing in left hanmi. Nage extends his left hand towards his partner's face. Uke brings her left hand up to meet nage's hand. Don't begin a contest of pushing against each other's hand. Simply have solid contact with each other.

Bend your knees to get a solid base and draw uke's head down to your left shoulder. Keep extending forward through your front hand to prevent her from turning towards you. Uke should begin losing her balance backwards.

Keep uke's head pinned to your shoulder. Nage's left arm makes a strong circle around uke's head. Turn your hips so that your arm feels as if it is an extension of your hip. Don't let your hip turn faster than the arm or your arm will become trapped behind you.

Step in deeply. Enter behind your partner with your left foot. The feeling is of surrounding your partner with your whole body and spirit. With your hand extending forward from your center, shift your weight forward and down, throwing your partner.

right   *wrong*

Be behind your partner. If your shoulders are in front of uke's shoulders, it will be a battle of power. Irimi means entering with your body.

right

For learning the principle of irimi/ entering in basic practice, hold the back of uke's collar. It is harder to control uke's body this way, and you will learn when your body is in the wrong position because uke will be able to easily rotate her shoulders and escape. Though it is easier to hold someone's neck or face or hair so that pain stops her from moving, you will learn little about irimi practicing this way. Once you can move your body confidently into irimi, how you hold won't matter as much.

If you pull uke's arm around, she can . . .

Do not drag uke's hand down and around towards you. This turns her body around and you end up face to face in a confrontation. If you bring her down, it can be difficult to bring her back up. Keep extending her arm forward so that her back remains rotated towards you.

escape.   *turn toward you and strike.*   *pull down on your arm.*

wrong ⟶

right ⟶

As you enter through uke to throw, keep your hands in front of your own center. If your hands wander from center even a bit, you will end up pulling uke through the technique.

Practice this static basic often. It is tempting to quickly move on to more exciting variations. The moment of entering happens in an instant. If you are not exquisitely familiar with the moment and place of joining with uke, then irimi will be reduced to dragging your partner to the mat. Practice this basic form slowly and carefully.

KI-NO-NAGARE

When you begin the fluid practice of irimi-nage, continue to enter with clarity. Though this practice feels very graceful, don't lose the "shinken" (sharp) spirit.

The form of irimi-nage remains the same as the static version. Elongate the motion slightly so that you don't shortcut any moves. Begin slowly, without stopping. Remember, you are adding the aspect of timing to the form, not changing it.

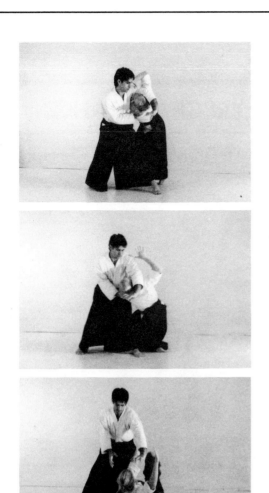

VARIATIONS

At the beginning of practice in irimi-nage, when uke attacks, nage gets out of harm's way and blends by stepping behind uke. In later stages the quality of the technique is that of already being behind uke at the moment she even considers striking.

Once the basic irimi-nage is understood deep within you, infinite variations on the technique will begin to appear. Each is an expression of the basic principle of irimi and stays true to it. Remember, a severe technique has the heart of compassion. A fluid technique has the soul of a sword.

The source of these techniques is in the basic form. If something feels wrong while practicing irimi-nage, the mistake is most likely in your understanding of the basic form. Find the mistake there and it will at the same time be corrected in the advanced form.

DIRECT ENTRANCE

Imagine the basic irimi-nage to be a photo slide. It can be blown up for detailed study or, as in this direct practice, it can be reduced to microfilm. None of the information is lost. It is just smaller.

UKE IS DOING A SHOMEN STRIKE

If uke's hand is already striking down, don't put your hand up to stop its motion. Move your body deeply behind her and turn completely sideways. This posture is called "hitoe mi."

Be careful not to leave your hand in the path of her strike.

Immediately bring your front shoulder close to uke; then continue to enter as in the basic technique.

NOTEBOOK

Don't block her strike.

right

Don't leave your hand in front of the strike.

ENTERING DEEPLY

This practice exaggerates the first entrance and hip turn. It is a superb practice for getting the feeling of being deep behind your partner. Enter behind uke as in the basic form.

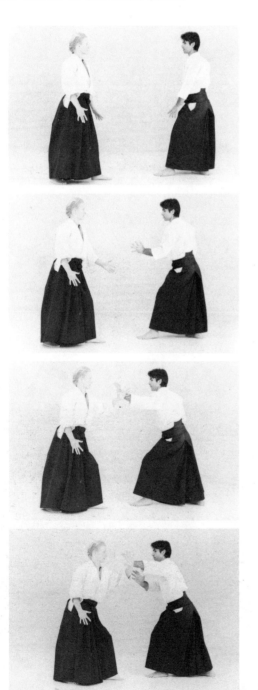

Drop very low and continue turning towards uke. Hold her collar and press forward and up on her back with your right forearm.

Extend up and forward with your front hand.
Uke's hips will move forward.

YAMABIKO NO MICHI

This variation has a nickname which means "Path of a mountain echo." When you yell in a mountain canyon, your voice goes out and is echoed back by the mountain.

Extend your hand, body and spirit powerfully out towards your partner. She echoes your motion by bringing her hand up to block yours.

Just before your hands meet, move your hand down so she can't reach it, and step in back of her. This draws her body and spirit into the space you occupied, but you are now behind her.

Continue with irimi-nage as before.

KI-NO-NAGARE LONG FORM

This style of practice has two clear purposes. First, it enlarges the technique like a photographic print so that it may be studied in detail. Secondly, by turning you can throw uke in any direction you wish.

When you enter behind your partner, stay behind her. If you drag down on her hand she will turn towards you and can then counter you or escape easily. To stay behind her, use the hand on her collar to keep her head close to you and keep her extended forward with your front hand.

GLOSSARY OF COMMON AIKIDO TERMS

Aikido: AI = Harmony
KI = Spirit
DO = The Way or Path.

Way of Harmony with
the Spirit of the Universe

Ai-hanmi: Mutual stance. Partners stand facing one another with the same foot forward, i.e. right/right.

Aiki Jinja: Aiki Shrine. The shrine O'Sensei built in Iwama, Japan, honoring the spirit and the deities of aikido.

Atemi: A strike. Striking techniques.

Bokken: Wooden sword.

Budo: Warrior Way. The group of disciplines that simultaneously teach martial technique and guide mental and spiritual development.

Dan: Black belt rank.

Deshi: Student, pupil, disciple.

Dojo: Training hall.

Dosa: An exercise.

Gaeshi: To reverse.

Gi: Training uniform.

Gyaku-hanmi: Opposite stance. Partners stand with the opposite foot forward, i.e. right/left.

Hakama: A divided, pant-like skirt.

Hanmi: Triangular stance. Literally means "half body."

Hanmi Handachi: Nage (thrower) is kneeling and uke (attacker) approaches from a standing position.

Hantai: Opposite or reverse.

Hara: Lower abdomen; physical and spiritual center.

Irimi: To enter; entering.

Jiyu Waza: Free style practice.

Jo: Wooden staff.

Kaiten: To revolve or rotate.

Kamae: Stance.

Kata: Shoulder.

Kata: Pre-arranged exercise that teaches basic forms and principles.

Keiko: Practice session; training.

Ken: Japanese sword.

Ki: Spirit; the vital force of the body; Universal Energy.

Kiai: A piercing scream or cry that unifies all parts of the body and spirit.

Kihon: Basic form of a technique.

Ki-no-nagare: Fluid form of a technique.

Kokyu: Breath—energy/ki flow and the motions of the body unified by control of the breath.

Kokyu-Ryoku: The power harnessed through practice of kokyu.

Kumi-tachi: Advanced sword practices done with a partner.

Kumi-jo: Advanced jo practices done with a partner.

Kyu: Ranks below "dan" (black belt).

Ma-ai: The appropriate distance between uke and nage. Means "harmony of space."

Men: Face, head.

Musubi: Uniting, bonding.

Nage: Throw; the person who throws.

O'Sensei: "The Great Teacher." Morihei Ueshiba, Founder of Aikido.

Oyo-waza: Variations on basic technique.

Randori: Multiple person attack.

Rei: Salutation, bow.

Reigi: Etiquette.

Riai: Common, unified principles of sword, staff and body techniques.

Samurai: Military retainer (feudal period).

Sempai: Senior student.

Sensei: Teacher, instructor.

Seiza: Formal sitting posture.

Shiho: Four directions.

Shomen: Front of a dojo. Often there is a photo of the Founder. Also means front or top of head.

Suburi: A single movement using the ken or jo, done as a solo practice.

Suwari Waza: Techniques done from a sitting position.

Tachi-dori: Techniques of taking an opponent's sword.

Tai-jutsu: Body arts. The techniques of aikido done without weapons.

Take-musu-aiki: Term used by the Founder describing the advanced levels of aikido. The creation of aiki techniques from a thorough understanding of aiki principles.

Tanto: Knife.

Tao: Chinese: "Do," path, discipline.

Te: Hand.

Tegatana: Hand blade. Sword edge of the hand, located between the little finger and the wrist.

Tsuki: Thrust, punch.

Uchi: To strike.

Ueshiba, Morihei: Founder of aikido. O'Sensei.

Uke: "To receive." A person who receives an attack. Generally "uke" refers to the person being thrown.

Ukemi: The art of falling. "To receive through the body."

Ushiro: Back, behind, rear.

Waza: Technique.

Yokomen: Side of head.

Yudansha: Person holding black belt rank.

Zanshin: Unbroken spirit. The concentrated connection that remains with one's partner even after the throw has been completed.

NAMES OF BASIC ATTACKS

Gyaku te-dori: Cross hand grab, i.e. right to right.

Hiji-dori: Elbow grab.

Kata-dori: Shoulder grab.

Katate-dori: Wrist grab (same side).

Katate-dori-hantai: Cross hand grasp, i.e. right hand grasps opponent's right wrist. Same as gyaku te-dori.

Men-uchi: Strike to the head.

Morote-dori: Attack in which wrist is held with both hands.

Mune-tsuki: Chest or stomach strike.

Muna-dori: Lapel grab.

Ryote-dori: Attack in which both wrists are held.

Shomen-uchi: Strike to the top of the head.

Ushiro eri-dori: Collar grab from behind.

Ushiro hiji-dori: Elbows grabbed from the rear.

Ushiro Ryo-kata-dori: Both shoulders grabbed from behind.

Ushiro ryote-dori: Both wrists grabbed from behind.

Ushiro kubi-shime: Choking with one hand around the neck from the rear.

Ushiro dori: Rear bear hug.

Yokomen-uchi: Strike to the side of the head.

NAMES OF BASIC TECHNIQUES

Gokkyo: Fifth pinning technique.

Ikkyo: First pinning technique.

Irimi-nage: Entering technique.

Juji garumi: Crossed-arm throw.

Kaiten-nage: Rotary throw.

Kokyu-dosa: Seated kokyu exercise.

Kokyu-nage: Breath throw. Often used for techniques that do not have a specific name.

Koshi-nage: Hip throw.

Kote-gaeshi: Wrist twisting technique.

Nikkyo: Second pinning technique.

Sankyo: Third pinning technique.

Shiho-nage: Four direction throw.

Sumi-otoshi: corner drop throw.

Tai-no-henko: Basic blending practice.

Tenchi-nage: Heaven-and-earth throw.

Yonkyo: Fourth pinning technique.

BASIC DIRECTIONS
OF A THROW

Omote-waza: Technique which goes forward or to uke's front.

Ura-waza: Technique which goes around or behind uke.

Irimi: Entering (same as Omote-waza).

Tenkan: Turning (same as Ura-waza).

NOTE:

The whole name of a technique in Japanese is formed by the word for the attack, then technique, then direction, e.g.,

attack	technique	direction.
shomen-uchi	ikkyo	omote-waza.
katate-dori	shiho-nage	ura-waza